Walks with Northampton U3A

by Howard D Richards

Also, by Howard D Richards

Snapshots in Time 1, (2014)
Brief Encounters, (2015)
Snapshots in Time 2, (2015)
Romania, (2016)
Greece, (2016)
Snapshots in Time 3, (2017)
Islands of the Tyrrhenian Sea, (2017)
Snapshots in Time 4, (2018)
Adventures in Turkey, (2018)
Travels through Italy, (2018)
A short Collection of prose and Poetry, (2018) and updated are Interesting Times (2020)
Blue Remembered Hills, a second collection of prose & poetry (2020)
Arcady Lost or Found? a third collection of prose and poetry (2020)
Times they're a-Changin, a fourth collection of prose and poetry (2021)

ISBN : 9798752851834
Imprint: Independently published

To Chris & Clive Spinney who led the Ramblers and Striders Group and who provided the opportunities for much pleasure over a period of my life.

Howard D Richards November 2021

After a day's walk, everything has twice its usual value.

G.M. Trevelyan

A walk in nature walks the soul back home

Mary Davis

I took a walk in the woods and came out taller than trees

Henry David Thoreau

Of all the paths you take in life, make sure a few of them are dirt

John Muir

Walking is feeling free of daily stresses and opens eyes to the wonders of the world. I have included poems and prose for both the Ramblers, Striders and Strollers groups of the U3A, for they reflect the experiences that Clive and Chris created for me. Unfortunately, many of walks in my early days with Clive and Chris were unrecorded and although some short articles were done for the U3A Newsletter under Jo Dumhof these have been lost to me. Some poetry was composed in my head at time of walking and never got written, yet maybe influenced other poetry of mine. Hopefully the poetry and prose set out within this book does reflect walking with Clive and Chris.

Howard D Richards

November 2021

Preface

I am not sure when Cicely and I joined the U3A Ramblers, but I was in my sixties and still working on contracts for the European Commission. It was Jean and Mike Angersen, who were friends of Cicely and myself, that introduced us to our first walk and Clive and Chis made us truly welcome. We had been told that the walks were always over a distance of '4.5 Miles', so were easy for us, as we were both very fit.

In those early years I thoroughly enjoyed the 'Ramblers', - walking fast, out in front, and at many times waiting for others to catch up. The walks too made it easy to make many new friends. There was Elizabeth and Alan Walker, Debbie and Dereck Hucker, whom we later went on holidays with, starting when three of us were seventy going to Amsterdam to celebrate. Further holidays followed in Strasbourg and the environs, Paris, Canterbury and Kent and Norwich and Norfolk. Other new found friends were Tony and Marilyn Sherwood. Tony was great fun always getting up to pranks on the walks, and Marilyn led the Strollers group, which we also joined. Through them met Roger and Linda Jackson and all had a great time at the first holiday arranged by Chris and Clive in Derbyshire. Later enjoyed many holidays throughout Europe with Linda and Roger, resulting in my travel books written afterwards.

There were also many other friends made as a consequence of the Ramblers Group and Joanna Domhof was one of these who changed my life. I had been persuaded by her to write short articles about the month's Ramble for the Northampton U3A Newsletter for which she was the editor. Eventually she convinced me to join the 'Scribbles' Creative Writing Group at Market Marborough that she was also a member of. During the time with them I started writing poetry, my first poem in the year I was 72.

The are always many characters in the walking group and in those early years remember one couple who outstripped everyone in their walking ability. He was a former fell runner and his wife of Sicilian origin. I can't remember their names, but the holiday in Derbyshire showed up their ability, often out in front taking the wrong path and having to make a rapid catchup manoeuvre to get out in front again, at times quite amusing.

During those walks that Clive and Chris organised, Clive always had his clip board for checks on people, activities and time targets. Often on the coach we would stop for a convenience break. Tony Bishop though always seized the opportunity to get a pint from the pub, even though it was a short break and on one memorable occasion Joy, his wife, dragged him out of the pub by the scruff of his neck still holding his pint, to get him back on the waiting coach. There were many incidents that gave me a laugh that happened during that holiday that added to the enjoyment.

As I have said I was a fast walker of which there were others too and persuaded Clive to create the 'Striders' group. Our first walk I remember was pleasant, although saved by Clive from disaster. The person leading it was a well-seasoned walker in the national Ramblers. It was after the first hour and a half that some of us said that we had been here before and it dawned on the leader that he had forgotten the way. To our relief Clive had a map that he always carried and sorted us out, but returned to the starting pub about an hour late having walked probably ten miles.

In more recent times Brian Adams has been an outstanding character, at all times very helpful, outspoken and at times entertaining with his colourful and sparkling outfits. Particularly, at Christmas time he was always great fun. He helped me a lot during my period of foot pain and subsequent to my foot operation that left me with four steel pins in it leaving me unable to walk fast again, or indeed lead walks as a consequence.

Now in my middle eighties and with the Covid breaks to the walking calendar I am left a shadow of my former self, and likely to be a 'tail end Charlie' for the Ramblers and no longer able to contemplate joining a Striders outing, much as I would like too. Nevertheless, the group gives me much pleasure and I still have the Strollers group to continue with.

Clive and Chris have provided an opportunity to see corners of the county and neighbouring ones that otherwise would have been missed and I thank them whole heartedly for this. Moreover, their holidays in Derbyshire, the Cotswolds and Shropshire were a delight. Within this book there are snapshot descriptions of some of the experiences through poetry or prose.

Poetry from walks within the Compass of Northampton

'All truly great thoughts are conceived while walking'

Friedrich Nietzsche

"The open road is beckoning, a strangeness, a place where man can lose himself"

William Least Heat Moon

"We wander for distraction, but travel for fulfilment"

Hilaire Belloc

Circular Walk around Lower and Upper Harlestone Northamptonshire

By the trees, snowdrops flower,

White clumps beneath the bower,

Houses cluster below the knoll,

To where we take a laid-back stroll,

Ironstone buildings we admire,

Some of the best in the shire;

Taking paths across the meadows,

In which old trees spread their shadows,

To arrive at the Fox and Hounds,

Where the lunchtime menu astounds

March 18th 2014 A poem conceived while walking with the U3A Strollers Group in Billing. Surprised by the amount of litter and rubbish in hedgerows and along wooded ways. Used extracts from William Blakes poem to emphasis

Behaviour in the New Society

'..In England's green and pleasant land',

Wrote an awe inspired William Blake,

Nowadays would he understand?

The tidy living, we forsake

A throw-away society

In the present-day plastic age

No end to the depravity

Even those who try to assuage

Bags full of dog shit hang from trees,

Cans of yellow piss tossed away,

'Take-Away' cartons spread disease,

Used condoms dumped, not gone astray

Frayed bags flutter in the hedgerows,

Discarded settees lie in ditches,

No surprises, anything goes,

These are the litterbug's riches

And did the Countenance Divine,

Shine forth upon our piles of waste?

And was Jerusalem buildéd here,

Among these green pastures defaced?

An Autumnal Walk

On a distant hill, harvesting long over,

Where, stubble glints silver in morning sunshine

Here and there brushed shadow from a passing cloud,

Greets another glorious autumnal day

Before me sparkling sprays of droplets erupt

As I trudge the dewy meadow grasses

Leaving distinct footprints in my clumsy wake

Surrounded by many clear bright spiders-webs

Their earlier invisibility switched

Now downhill towards the steep river valley

Where gnarled old oaks have turned buttery yellow

Complimenting neighbouring dark russet greens

Set off with a scattering of red maple

Careful now of hedgerows full of thorny briars

Deadly tangles with ripe black shiny berries

Intermingled with bright orange red rosehips

Food for hungry field mice and turdidae

Beyond the rise an ancient village loom's,

Where black-faced sheep leisurely graze their pasture,

And rooks with black baggy trousers squawk from tall trees,

But there at last the welcome of the local inn

February 27th 2015, with the U3A 'Ramblers' Group at Upper Stowe, but didn't go with them because of an injured right foot, but walked around the village trying to sketch instead. The wind was cool, the sky clear blue, but too cold for sketching. Went back to the 'Old Dairy' and the restaurant there to drink morning coffee as well as writing the following poem about my surroundings.

At the Dairy: Upper Stowe

Down in the valley bottom

Skeletal trees are budding

Ageless winter forgotten

Soon green leaves will be shooting

But the wind blows cool across the hill

Where old desiccated plants, grey-white

Stand forlornly waiting summer still

Hoping of warm days full of light

The Kune pig and rams chomp the grasses

In the spongy meadow wet from rain,

Kicking up blackened earth, dark masses,

Where corvins come to feed yet again

The neighbouring church nestles on the rise

Yew shadowed, a place of solitude

Where crosses mark the spot of man's demise,

As part of religious rectitude

I sit looking out from the old barn

Warmed by a log fire, red embers bright

Sipping coffee, contented, keeping calm,

My companions now out of sight

Enjoying their walk from Upper Stowe

Under a bright cerulean sky,

Vast vistas of landscape endow

With woods and hills that can make you cry,

What a wonderful world

Before us all unfurled

March 14th 2015, a dry and sunny day with a cold wind blowing in from the east. Having just finished my piece on 'Wellbeing' for the U3A sources magazine wrote the following poem,

Walking to Happiness

The rolling pastures with distant spires,

A glorious landscape, one never tires,

Hedgerows whitened with blackthorn flowers,

Buttery celandine in bowers,

Mewling buzzards high in the heavens,

Partridges all sixes and sevens

With our approaching swish through grasses

And a piercing snap of dead branches

Walking, feeling free and energized

Such exquisiteness, am mesmerized

Sharing with others nature's allure

Magical lighting in shafts so pure

Illuminating thatched cottages

In shades of gold and burnt oranges,

Nearby the sign for the village inn

And the friendly atmosphere within

Glowing healthy faces all round seeing,

Talking, discussing full of wellbeing

March 19th 2015, dry with white cloud cover with a cold wind blowing in from the east.

Foggy Day

Can't see through the thick white fog

That came in the cold dark night

Blocking everything from sight

Blanketing the river valley

From above brilliant brightness

Below all dimness and wetness

Plodding onwards through the murk

Seeing looming bare branched trees

Dripping sodden, - still, no breeze

Trousers clinging, drenched through grasses

Droplets dripping from my hoody

The infernal fog so broody

Escape into the lit café

Getting away from dreariness

Where hot soup stems the weariness

March 29th 2015, rain showers from the west, thinking about last Friday's U3A ramble from Cosgrove when I could only walk a little because of my bad right foot

Canal Walk

Along the Grand Union canal

The walk stimulating my morale

Where carpets of sweet white violets hide

Amongst grasses by the water side

Narrow boats being primed for Eastertide

Maybe I could be taken for a ride,

But sadly, my luck is not in today,

As nobody's free to take me away

To glide down the waterway being free

A genuine veritable escapee

From my trying somatic limitations

Thinking of those likely destinations

Instead,I plod back to the Barley Mow,

A delightful pub I will not forgo

Where I will meet with others at lunchtime,

Pondering on those fair violets in sunshine

Successful Walk with the U3A

A chilly morning setting off from Houghton,

Almost forty of us braving the cold breeze

On the outlying fringes of Northampton,

Through the trees my foot improving by degrees,

Following the course of the old Bedford line,

Bare of flowers not even a celandine,

Through the maze of an industrial estate

And over the River Nene Navigation,

Passing by the Britannia, all sedate,

The walk goes well, a minor celebration.

Through more stark trees around the Premier Inn

- To emerge where vast open skies begin,

The river flood reliefs, dykes and waterfowl,

All in the melancholy valley landscape,

Where at night time red foxes and badgers prowl,

And all geese sleep on lake islands to escape.

Leaving the others to take a short cut back

I walk by the Hardingstone Embankment track,

See St Mary the Blessed Virgin's tall spire,

Needle shaped on the faraway village hill,

Grey silhouettes across the water retire,

My friends take a coffee break, but it's cold still,

We will meet later at the warm friendly inn

Where we will take our lunch and drinks within.

Down a bank through a gate by way of a trail

To tread my way through an unexciting field

To at last, have a long hill to assail,

Where my last vestiges of strength are revealed,

But arrive at last at the Old Cherry Tree

Where the barman provides me with good coffee

April 29th 2016, I promised Eileen Brown a poem for the U3A magazine for the Ramble that took place from West Haddon at the end of April.

Walk to Winwick

From Pytchley Inn West Haddon,

Taking the Jurassic Way,

Into wind with chills full on,

Despite a sunny spring day,

Approach the hamlet of Winwick,

Passing by the watermill house,

Tall, imposing, built of red brick,

Probably home to a country mouse

An ancient place, Doomsday records,

Home to Sir Thomas Mallory,

One of the medieval lords,

Morte d'Arthur famed Allegory,

Church of Michael and all Angels,

With New Millennium Stained-Glass,

Now in national treasure tables,

But no mention of Cromwell, alas.

The village a former haven,

For many eloping couples,

Married before a maiden taken,

The church congregation chuckles;

Leave at last absorbing Winwick,

Past a Jacobean Manor,

With curved boundary walls of brick,

To a landscape of glamour,

The upland rolling rounded hills,

Of glorious Northamptonshire,

Fields of ridge and furrow instils,

Contentment, beauty to admire,

A path takes us past White House Farm,

Encountering a shaggy pony,

And other beasts that caused no harm,

To lunch at the pub, - all agree.

August 11th 2016, exploring the U3A Stroll for the next Monday on a hot and sunny day.

Olney to Emberton Park

Huge fluffy white cumulus, decorate a sapphire sky,

As I set out one superb August morning from Olney,

An ancient town by the Great River Ouse that passes by,

A stream that flows to far off Eastern Wash with impish glee;

Pass near to the Gothic church of St Peter and St Paul,

Where a bygone curate-poet composed 'Amazing Grace',

And to the crossing where Prince Rupert in a well fought brawl

With militia retreated when warned of Cromwell's wild chase.

Into Emberton Park to stroll with others of like mind,

Where there are attractive lakes formed from former gravel pits,

And pathways for those frazzled mums with pushchairs, to unwind,

Also for joggers, Sunday cyclists and other keep fits;

The walk, through trees by ruffled waters, is simply pleasing,

But in time find access to the long-distance river way

That follows the river to the far sea, meandering,

Passing through Bedfordshire and Black Fenland to King Lynn's quay.

Across the water on the ridge a long line of houses,

Mixed together all shapes and sizes, many colours too,

The track follows the riverbank beyond verging sedges,

Under rustling leaves of old field maples that scatter light;

Towards the distant towering spire of the aforesaid church,

Leading back to the snug, busy, bustling community,

Where take refreshment at the Two Brewers, no need
to search,

A good inn to take beer, given the opportunity.

July 20th 2016, poem written after a U3A Stroll

Walgrave to Hannington

A hot summer's day with high white wispy cloud,

Strolled through a wheat field, humid, ripening fast,

Taking a path, Walgrave to Hannington,

Over worn old stiles and green land unploughed,

Where, ancient grazed ridge and furrow holdfast,

Retaining in memory stories homespun,

The church St's Peter and Paul and lost inns,

A close-knit village, mellow stone houses,

Huddled, quiet, unassuming, tree shaded,

Old England lost in time, with hidden sins.

Wakening from deep thought consciousness rouses,

But marks on the landscape have never faded,

Dreaming, drifting, leisurely returning,

Going back to the valley for lunch

At the Royal Oak, its inn sign painted

With a latter-day smiling Prince Charming,

Interestingly it's not what packs the punch

It's St George slaying the Dragon, untainted.

January 19th 2016, I had been out with the U3A Strollers to Harlestone Firs, I managed the two and half miles through the woods pretty well and it gave me confidence for walking on rough ground again.

First Strollers 2016

Quiet steady steps through Harlestone Firs,

Under foot leaves rustling,

Fallen branches crunching,

See through the sentinel tree trunks

Patches of gleaming snow,

Winter's adagio,

Carefully looking for hidden gems,

Snowdrops, or primroses,

Seen under our noses.

The path snakes on into the depths,

Narrow, watching branches,

All entangling arches,

Until we emerge in a field,

A grassy bridleway,

Muddy, to our dismay,

Ahead more bare woods to pass through,

More mud, the path twists on,

All the snow here long gone,

Out onto an exposed hillside

Above the Nene valley,

The view makes me happy.

Returning through the trees once more,

An achievement for me,

How far next time, we'll see.

February 18th 2016, a poem written after my second long stroll while recovering from my foot operation

Stroll from Windhover and Back

Walked along beside the railway track,

Where shabby engines in sidings lay,

That some enthusiasts may bring back

With various adornments they say,

Past a station open on Sundays

For Northampton and Brampton rail rides,

Just a short length of track to appraise,

With remembrances and fun besides,

Recollecting renowned days of steam,

A branch line to Market Harborough,

- Sadly, now no more than a dream,

Due to Beeching, his job was thorough.

We walk on to Merry Tom crossing,

Where another station will be built,

Not far from a long-buried coffin,

And a monument for an Earl's guilt,

Merry Tom was a fine hunting horse,

Belonging to Spencer the Red,

Failed to jump the river Nene, of course,

Ended up with a broken neck, dead

But his name lives on through a lane

And in time a handsome station sign.

At the crossing gate turned back again,

To the Windhover to drink red wine

Walk from Great Houghton

Left the Cherry Tree Great Houghton

Eastwards heading

Over frozen uneven fields

Heavy treading

Down through rambling Little Houghton

Towards the Nene,

Taking the footpath to Billing

To turn again

Along the river to the flats,

Around the lake

And back up hill to Great Houghton

For luncheon break

March 22nd 2017 a very wet day for our walk with U3A Strollers.

March Strollers 2017

Wary of the mid-March weather,

Changeable, expectant showers,

Our walk couldn't have been wetter,

Chose the stormy downpour hours

Ended soaked through to boxer shorts

Shirt and my backpack wet, so stripped,

Dried off, surrounded by good sports,

Then dressed as is social prescript

In the village pub in dry clothes,

Sat with others still soaking wet,

Enjoying beer in calm repose,

After chewed on a stuffed baguette

Ramble to Great Doddington and Back

Out from Great Doddington down the Nene Valley
Way,

Across lush green grassy fields

Looking at the quiet river stretching west to east,

A magical view it yields

Winding silvery blue with adjacent numerous lakes,

In the wide pleasant valley,

Amongst many trees and shrubs, and other
vegetation,

We walk and look not dally

Crossing the old valley railway course to Summer
Leys,

A bird sanctuary on a lake,

Where swans, geese and ducks and other waterfowl
commute,

To stop for a minor break

There, at a hide, watched bullfinches and chaffinch's
feed,

Dressed in their bright mating hues,

Before continuing on to cross where waters

Of canal and river fuse

Then on uphill back to the long strung-out village

Admiring the spring blossom,

Blackthorn and Pussy Willow decorating hedgerows,

The view behind still awesome

Eventually returned to the Stagshead for lunch,

To celebrate spring together

With beer and wine and ample tasty repast,

Thankful for the pleasant weather

Summer Lanes

Along by hedgerows lit by morning light,

Chaffinches and yellow hammers calling,

Verges full of nature's wildest delight

Some upright to the sun, others sprawling;

There's purple mallow and off-white yarrow,

Called 'Old Man's Baccy', to user's sorrow

Cranesbill crawls through the feathered grasses,

Clover and bindweed by open spaces

And rambling pea-like dense bushy vetches

Grow with moon daisies with open faces.

A robin from a high branch sings loudly

Puffing his pink russet breast out proudly

Numerous beautiful flowers yet to see

Bright yellow patches of bird's foot trefoil,

Pink racemes of sainfoin I spy with glee

And pale blue flax that from their seeds comes oil,

Also not forgetting the meadow sweet,

In great quantity it's always a treat.

Quiet English country lanes are a palette,

Splashing out surprising variety

Of colours seductive as a soubrette,

Throughout different grasses with gaiety.

These hidden places are now uncommon,

But can still find them, they're not forgotten

Walk to Faxton

Left White Horse at Old through fields of corn

Towards Faxton on a lonely hill,

The missing village of which we mourn

For which passing time didn't stand still

There in a corner of a rape field

A tiny dark wood of conifers,

But inside a tangled mess revealed

Within tall weeds and nettle stingers

An abandoned dark fenced enclosure.

At its centre a sad looking stone,

An old font aged by time exposure;

Why here forgotten and all alone?

Except for overgrown broken walls,

Near to crepuscular woodland edge,

A tragedy that few now recalls

A wanton destruction, some allege.

It's all that remains of St Denis

Demolished in 1958,

By a shameless philistine menace,

What's left experts tried to expiate

A relic from many broken bits

Restored by great artists in three years

For the V&A, where it now sits,

A large relief in alabaster

Remembering Sir Augustine Nicholls,

Who died in 1647,

That the fine memorial extols

With model angels, - from heaven

After the old church was demolished

Very last of the villagers left

Its place in modern life was finished,

Bulldozed, ploughed up, only a few wept.

Lasted a thousand years, now farmland

With an occasional poignant stone.

With no roads you start to understand.

Walked back down through ripened rape alone

August 30th 2017, the poem below encompasses many experiences of walks in the summer

Late Summer Walk

Heat already felt,

As morning mists cleared away

From ground where I dwelt,

To be another fine day

Crunching across fields

Thick with sharp flaxen stubble,

Stands from harvest yields,

Stuff of late summer's ramble

Where running brown hares

Chase across to distant trees

By brambles in pairs,

Scampering faster by the lee's

Shiny blackberries

In juicy hanging bunches,

Fruits for the faeries

And many bird relishes

Leaving straw strewn land

To harrowed and ploughed spaces

Russet browns expand

Signs of autumn's embraces

A darkened vastness

Stretching to far horizons,

Where skies caress

The closing corrugations

Circling birds prepare

For long onward migrations

To fly south elsewhere,

For new summer vacations

Down by the hedge walk

Thick with sloes and other fruits,

Where a crow offers a squawk

From an old tree with gnarled roots

A farmer ploughing,

Followed by clouds of seagulls

For worms endowing,

In many high screeching calls

Northwards the forest,

Covering hillsides in grim greens,

Hues of late August

Starting the Fall's in-between's

Tucked in a hollow

Lies a quiet huddled village,

There's a track to follow,

Part of ancient heritage

Where Saxon serfs trod

On the way to sing in church

Worshiping their god

And their consciousness search

Close, Tumble-Down Dick,

An inn that welcomes strangers,

Serene in its old red brick,

Free from marauding dangers

There imbibe with ale

Brewed locally with fine hops,

Bronzed liqueur, not pale,

Always served with frothy tops

Perhaps too, have a pie,

Water crust pastry and pork,

Jelly to satisfy

With hot mustard on your fork

Depart homely place,

Contented and satisfied,

Take steps to retrace

Wonderful, pride in my stride

27th November 2017 a poem written after a Ramble.

Walk from Grendon

Plodding feet strung out in a ribbon astern,

Conversation fluid, catching an odd word.

Delight, of muddy patches there's no concern,

Vast landscapes stretch out their clarity un-blurred,

See over the valley to far Northampton.

Descend a slope below the ridge at Grendon,

Distant Castle Ashby house lit by the sun,

A pheasant stirred with sounds like a Gatling gun,

Below lakes shimmer silver where anglers wait.

A long wide field to cross, new crops showing green,

Thick mud gathers on boots, fluidity frustrate,

Heavier going to reach a lane now seen,

Walk up hill to reach the winding Yardley Road

And there turned south westward for a bridal track,

To go eastward away from my true abode

Heading to far Easton Maudit with the pack.

Stood by the hamlet's stream for light snacks and
drinks

By a thatched cottage with old tree gnarled posts,

Before the cohort moved onwards in high jinks.

Passing the church, old cedars and ancient ghosts,

Down to an abandoned barn, tall weeds within,

Then through fields aiming for Grendon church tower,

To be soon settled in at the Half Moon Inn

For lunch, after noon at half past the hour

Winter Senses

The scents of morning

Earthy after rain,

And the day dawning,

No one can complain

They lift the spirits

And all have merits

On through wet grasses

Soaking trouser legs,

- no surprises,

With foul grungy dregs

From winter ploughing

And slurry spreading

Get to the hill top

See for many miles.

For a while I stop

Seeking footpath stiles

For the way ahead

Finding the track's thread

Progress slowly now,

Boots picking up mud

From an erstwhile plow

And is the lifeblood

Of winter walking,

Frequent boot cleaning

Back on meadow land,

Alongside a copse,

Where dense hazels stand.

Dangling from their tops

Bright golden flowers,

Catkins in bowers

On through the dark wood,

Tripping over roots

In all likelihood

With my muddy boots,

But have no concern,

As I twist and turn

Emerge safe, intact,

Into strong sunshine,

Different views distract,

Running hares, divine,

Across a green hill

Lovely sight, just brill

Continue ahead,

Downhill to a stream,

Following the thread

The water agleam,

Not a sound, peaceful,

A scene pure blissful

From a bridge looking,

Seeing coots in reeds

And mallards paddling,

In amongst the weeds

Brown and battered

Somewhat bedraggled

Traversing the bridge

Went towards the west

Up to a long ridge

And at the high crest

Looked to villages

With snug cottages

Smoke spiralled upwards

Sign of winter's cold,

Carry on homewards

In a hillside fold

- At peace with life,

No longer at strife

Post Viral Long Walk

Set out from Elwes Arms Great Billing

Towards the Nene following a stream

Through trees until emerged in rubbish

Scattered across the ground, just hellish,

Even dangling from a smooth hornbeam,

The whole tragic scene just appalling;

A mess, pressed on cogitating

Those filthy habits in extreme.

Under a bridge towards the Nene

Through Billing's large caravan park

Saw a woman chasing a dog.

Dressed in a pink rabbit suit agog.

Smiled as we passed by the lark

With words by some comedienne.

On past more grey trailers again,

Dismal, quiet, not even a bark.

By a bridge over the river

Came to a muddy field of rape,

Sticky yellow clay stuck to boots.

Climbed through two fields treading the roots.

Reached Little Houghton to escape

Muddy menace did not dither,

But on through the streets manoeuvre

Until seeing a far townscape

Then took a footpath to descend,

To the valley bottom once more

By way of wet meadows attack

Before meeting a quaggy track

Not bothering with grime anymore

Walking to the sorrowful end

Through a trailer park to ascend

And through much rubbish as before

Returning to the Elwes Arms,

Exhausting uphill with tired legs,

Zombie like for the last half mile,

Others behind in single file

Using all my energy dregs.

At last, the inn with all its charms,

Warm and welcoming it transforms

By comforting what my spirit begs

A February Stroll with the U3A

A grey Monday stroll in February,

A few spots of rain, the sky dark pewter.

Started from the Walter Tull restaurant

A good place for our little monthly jaunt,

Avoiding any tardy commuter

Crossing Walter Tull Way being wary,

For speeding trucks and cars always scary,

Ware of odd vehicles honking their hooter

Walking down a steep ramp with balustrades

Such a playful place for a skateboarder,

Past Northampton Town football stadium

And a monument In Memoriam

To the Town's famous mixed-race footballer

Who, killed in action missed his salad days,

A brave officer who received much praise,

But suffered bigotry and rank order

Leaving behind memories of The Great War

Walked down sad rubbish strewn Duston Mill Lane

And on to the River Nene flood plain streams,

Over two bridges with weary daydreams

To Grand Union Canal waterway vein,

Now a redundant link from Blisworth sore.

Walked west along the towpath to explore

The foul rush clogged water, our pace sustain

Reaching quiet Rothersthorpe Road Bridge turned
back

To walk towards Sixfields, the landscape grey,

So dismal, walked longingly ahead.

Shortly crossed a steel bridge to where it led

Through Upton Country Park before midday.

In front terraced houses white and lilac,

Architecturally pleasing feedback

When walking along Clickers Drive pathway

Past Buddies, to Frankie and Benny's,

Then on uphill past a long lunchtime queue

Waiting in line for their Mc Donald's fix

Selecting from the menu to pick and mix,

We walked on past bidding them all adieu,

To return for our lunch expectancies,

Beer and fish and chips, the 'Codfather', jollies,

A pub meal very far from cordon bleu

Mallows Cotton

The morning air is warm and still,

As we set out from Woodford Mill

Along the old Nene railway trail

For the people, not network rail

Embankments returned to the wild

Mammon and nature reconciled.

The beauty of apple blossom,

And Hawthorne, soon to be awesome

By meandering Nene, I go,

See waters ripple far below,

And just after take the Raunds Way,

Seeing butterflies fly today

Across the flood plain by Hog Dyke,

Where four egrets take off, ghostlike,

Their spectral white forms flying high

Into the clear indigo sky

Many mauve-like cuckoo flowers,

Drew the orange tip through the hours.

See across the flowing waters

To where a lost village moulders,

There lies ancient Mallows Cotton,

In a field long time forgotten,

Just humps in a grassy meadow,

Highlighted by subtle shadow

When did it die out, no one knows,

Could have been the plague, I suppose,

Like other Medieval place

Covered over with little trace

Circular Walk from Lamport

A hot June day, not a cloud in the sky,

Soft blue, and distant hills the eye can see

Hazy, not well defined from rising heat.

Left Lamport Swan for the railway retreat,

Abandoned now in the western valley,

Only the track bed remains, some ask why,

Beeching of course so long ago, I sigh,

The future was difficult to foresee

Walked south along the Brampton Valley Way,

Through the shade of tall trees bounding the trail

Until Houghton crossing to take the road

Walking up hill our pace - somewhat slowed,

The heat and drag forcing us to assail,

Leaving the peak of Clint Hill to turn away,

To pass through the village without delay,

Leaving Hanging Houghton to a grander scale

For a short while south along the ridge road

Before taking a rough path East to Scaldwell,

Crossed a field of rape by treated line,

Weed killer reminding of insect life no sign,

Decimation for reasons who can tell,

Next through a field of high grasses went astray,

Our Leader not knowing it wasn't the entry,

Realised, came to and dropped a bombshell

It was back through compact vegetation

To find the proper way, a hidden stile,

Hedgerow covered, yet strangely inviting,

And full of fun for those shorter, clambering

Into a sunny field to dwell awhile

Where many butterflies gave elation,

So happy, walked on in celebration

Through the mown hay followed the rank and file

Soon came to Grange Farm seeing fine black sheep,

Two flocks one dark black the other burnt umber,

The latter with white face and tail features

In a meadow with two alert creatures,

Guarding, smart alpacas, far from slumber.

Went on through the village mostly asleep

Until northwest by a field footpath sweep

Let not thoughts of soft merriment cumber

Climbed in Time to a tree line at Lamport,

After passing through fields of ripened rape,

Then turned with leaden limbs for a long drink,

So hot and tired, of food I didn't think,

The pub not far in this wondrous landscape,

Plodding along no energy to cavort

Using my remaining strength to exhort

At last, the outlines of the Swan takes shape

Autumn Transition

Cooler mornings, dew on gossamer threads,

Sparkling in the morning sunlight like jewels

Amongst heaths and purple heathers spreads

And in those sylvan spaces, light pools

End of summer melancholy lingers,

A tail end of last dying promises,

Chestnut trees with fallen glossy conkers,

Blackberries withering in the hedges,

But it's the glorious night time event

On those clear cool days with brilliant stars,

In the east Orion's slow ascent

With nearby Jupiter, Venus and Mars,

It is a sign of approaching winter,

As hours of darkness steadily increase

And a time of the happy vintner

Making new wine, perhaps a masterpiece,

These are the autumnal days, glorious fall,

Leaves of muted shades of gold to crimson,

Swirl in miniature maelstroms, often recall

In an artist's perception and vision

Stowe February 2019

Enchanting wide vistas at Stowe

A park with temples and follies,

Hidden gems, patches of woodland,

Where fine snowdrops discretely stand

With pinkish cyclamen soirées;

Valley lakes, streams, hillside meadow

Where sheep graze, a pastoral show,

A scene of many allegories

Beyond a small wood lies Lamport,

Just sorry bumps in a meadow

All that is left of the village

Since aristocratic pillage,

One of three clearances at Stowe,

Its namesake and Boycott were sport,

Through dominance they did exhort,

The land saw no more use of plough

Walk from Arthingworth and Back Again

Drove north towards Kelmarsh through mist,

To emerge in full sunshine, blissed,

On to Arthingworth on its hill

A lovely place with daffodil

Started a walk from the Bull's Head

Passed where crocus and snowdrop spread

To follow the Oxendon road,

Near where Sidom's Ford River flowed

Reaching at last the Brampton Valley Way

Along which we walked with the ease of the day

Thinking of 'Harborough trains long ago

To and from Northampton firebox aglow

In the near distance a tunnel beckoned,

On through darkness, a quarter mile reckoned,

Emerging to a cutting to behold

Huffing and puffing like steam trains of old

Climbed out of the shade up a slippy-slope

Into the sunshine once more, full of hope

There in a meadow of ridge and furrow,

That has seen many years since the harrow,

Stood old stately bare of leaf chestnut trees

Their bald boughs bending to the ground at ease

And in the background snowdrops in white clumps

Contrasting to grey tones of the tree trunks

Plodded on through Great Oxendon village,

Adding little to the total mileage

Leaving Little Oxendon to the north

Now just a medieval ghost thenceforth

To slide and skid down to the deep cutting,

Back through the stygian tunnel strutting

Remembering trains with emerging whistle,

Wishing we were on that steam bound missile,

At the site of the old Clipston and Oxendon station

Turned to Arthingworth with expectation

- The road seemed long with a steady climb

The temperature feeling like summertime

Sapping energy to stand the incline

Knowing that in a short while we will dine

Arrived back at the Bull's Head tired but content,

The walk was an enjoyable event

Dynamics of light and Shade

Clouds hurrying across the sky

Cast fleeting soft shadows below

Dynamics of light and shade,

An illuminated landscape,

A natural theatre production,

A poetic performer's dream,

Sometimes captured by an artist

Wet Spring Weather

The storms have passed leaving all bedraggled,

A misty landscape devoid of colour,

Just soft focus, shades of grey, dishevelled,

The overall view couldn't be duller

When will late spring return to gladden hearts?

Puffy white cumulus in sapphire skies,

The countryside in a pallet of arts,

Discoveries of unexpected surprise

Such moments of revelation amaze,

A shock of understanding sheer splendour,

Such as, far-fields of red poppies ablaze

And close up their soft beauty surrender

Yet the dismal drenching rain comes again,

Overshadowed by a stygian gloom,

And through the many days it does maintain,

The Jet Streams ordeal to the edge of doom

Olney and Environs

Wandering by the River Ouse

Over cool grassland meadows

With wild flowers shining out,

Yarrow, hawkweed hereabout,

Where meandering water slows

Deep and dark it does bemuse,

A place where fishermen snooze,

And other animals, doze

Within the bend of the river,

Clifton Reynes, Newton Blossomville,

Those quiet villages hunker down.

Walk back to the small market town,

Famous for its pancake race still,

In spring Olney will deliver,

The place is a pleasure giver

At peace and with friendly goodwill

Famed for its romantic poet,

William Cowper, and others,

Like the lyricist John Newton,

Whose 'Amazing Grace' was number one,

But also famed for Prince Rupert's runners

A fight he could win, but blew it.

The Roundheads did wholly outwit

Ending as Olney rout winners

Silently now the Great Ouse flows

On its journey to the North Sea.

Olney has kept its character

Despite the MK commuter,

High Street and Market Square lively,

Its commerce and trade shows,

Flexible like river willows,

And a place for afternoon tea

Walk in the Snow

In the long white winter,

Meadows covered in snow,

Frosted birches glisten,

All quietness, just listen,

Any sounds dampened now.

Feel the cold it's bitter,

You're no townie quitter,

Even if the winds blow.

Plod on through obscure fields

Leaving distinct footprints,

Defining your fresh trail

With character detail,

Shadows with blueish hints,

In the way the snow yields

And deepened recess shields

With those darkening tints

See distant village lights,

Homely, beckoning delight,

Eggs you onward, intent,

Your energy near spent,

The tall church spire in sight

And the last stile by rights,

Charged with emotive heights

Onwards with coming night

At last seated by fire,

settled in its warm glow,

Comfy, contented, now,

Walked the six miles somehow,

The cold sapped my strength though,

With snow across the shire,

Now sleep comes, my desire,

Thermal passions bestow

January Blues

A woodland of tall bleak bare trees,

With some conifers showing green

Dripping with the sad mists of time

Refreshing sorry winter's slime,

A melancholic brooding scene

That provides feeling of unease

And with a real wish to appease

What the deep gloominess may mean

Summer Leys

The lake silver black with sparkling ripples

Seen through stands of coppiced hazel and ash.

Where scrapes show ducks, geese and black
cormorants.

The river Nen with fast flowing currents,

Seeing at the weirs a white-water splash

Ringing loudly out like Grandsire triples

Noisily across fallow field stipples,

As the fast river waters dash and thrash

Walk the old railway track glancing through trees,

Bare dark silhouettes, to the sombre lake,

Hear birds singing, shrill trills of the blackbirds,

Full of mimicry, details have no words,

Magically going on since morning break.

Onwards, taking all in at Summer Leys

The enchantment, my feelings full at ease

Yet all my senses now fully awake

Summer Greenways

Walking the greenways of early summer,

Ancient hedgerows full of lucent delights,

As the dog rose, its thorny fronds wander,

Scrambling with pink and white to those lustrous
heights

A deep sweet scent exudes at eventide

From this old plant once known as eglantine.

Other plants to admire at the wayside

Have flowers in clusters in forms divine,

The elderflower and common dogwood,

The former with white frothy corymbs

And the latter like neat trim saucer hoods

At the end of green leafy stiff branched limbs.

Then by grassy footfalls through moon daisies,

White petals surround a yellow floret.

Faces point skywards like dainty ladies

Feathery leaves though show a different aspect.

These old country byways give much pleasure

To chance upon the unexpected

On those startling days you always treasure

That in time will be recollected

Nene Way Walk with Kubla Khan

Along a path on a wet day,

Left cars behind to Becket's Park,

Keeping to riverside green splay

Under bare trees with dripping bark

Going on under Becket's Bridge

To where moored narrow boats began,

Thinking of Samual Coleridge,

'Where Alph, the sacred river, ran'

Keeping to the Nene riverside

Pressed onwards passing by swans,

And on by houses in my stride,

The balconies shining like bronze

The poem went on, in my head,

'With walls and towers were girdled round',

Factories and walkways, to shops led

By the river there was no sound

Up a rise, Cattle Market Road,

Crossed it and Bridge Street to go on

Once more to where the river flowed,

Thinking again of Kubla Khan

Walking on by Carlsberg brewery

To dark Darlington Brook to cross,

'A stately pleasure dome decree',

An arching footbridge full of moss

'Where was held the mingled measure?'

From over the river bank sounds

Hearing distant calls of pleasure

From Aldi shoppers doing their rounds

Then on under the Towcester Road

Passing backends of industry

Their grey and dismal outlook showed

Exclaiming lack of artistry

Passed the railway a change of scene

To where the flowing river splits,

Sixfields Reservoir in between,

And a choice of walking circuits

To which Kubla Khan did entice

'For he on honey-dew hath fed

And drunk the milk of Paradise'

Content, no longer walked ahead

Walk from Great Brington

Shadows on the church wall

Dancing flickering light.

The last walk can't recall

From the pandemic plight

People in the graveyard

Remembering many names,

Retrieval sometimes hard,

Was it Dick, was it James?

Reminiscing, walking

A path to kissing gate,

As I strolled on talking

Into Althorp estate

Through the 'Alley' downhill,

An avenue of trees,

Their spring like greens just brill',

No longer ill at ease

At the lined stone walled park,

Distant Earl's house stood out

And fallow deer so dark,

The rarer black, no doubt

Through fields straight as arrow,

Muddy into meadow,

Over ridge and furrow,

Rain lashed down like gusto

Wet, yet happy, pressed on,

Rain stopped, drying slowly.

At old Lower Brington

Ironstone houses please me

Their rusty brown ochres

Giving aged worn charm

And the warmth it nurtures,

Quiet place that does no harm

Then back to Great Brington

Where Saint Mary's church stands

Lit with the midday sun

And beyond the grasslands

This hilly countryside,

Magic gem of the Shire,

That you walk through with pride

And landscape to admire

Obelisk Trail

A masculine statement standing tall,

An Obelisk, on a wooded hill,

Strolled down through trees on the northern side

A rounded wide-open landscape eyed.

On past a field of barley, green still,

Where wildflowers alongside hedgerows sprawl

White Campion and Moon Daisies enthral,

Ever onwards there was more to thrill

Across a downward slope, swathes of red,

From Flanders poppies in their splendour

And below a line of shapely trees

Our senses heightened by degrees.

Downhill, through leafy glen, no surrender.

By Boughton Brook, a dark rippling thread,

To go up a gentle rise ahead,

Where pink wild roses looked so tender

Came to a road where large houses stood

Magnificent in plush surroundings

And walked on to old Boughton village,

Ashley House, its gargoyles looked vintage,

But beyond the gates no skeleton riding.

Rusty ironstone cottages looked good.

Walked past houses up to the dark wood

Back to the obelisk for homecomings

Honeysuckle

Searching along the lane, discovering

Heavy with perfume of honeysuckle,

That rambles intriguingly through hedges

Golden jewels matched by ruby bright roses

That you reach to touch with dew on knuckle,

Hands miss many spider's webs, hovering,

Avoiding sweetbriar thorns, not touching,

To trailing woodbine nectar, to suckle

U3A Walkers

Walking with the U3A once more,

A happy band plodding slowly ahead

Across meadow grasses, through ploughed straw,

By woodlands and along canals in awe

Of adorned narrow boats, as we tread,

Reading their novel names with flair galore,

Then back to country routes since days of yore,

Overgrown with nettles and brambles spread

Joys of pushing through avoiding root trips

Getting scratched and stung, clay sticking to boots,

All this taken in stride of seasoned walkers,

Cool and unfazed the social talkers,

Fortitude, tolerance, their attributes,

Ultimate goal focused on beer foamed lips

And perhaps a lunch of fish and chips

At a welcome inn of good reputes

July 31st 2016, Brian Adams was there at the U3A Ramble, dressed in shorts, rather extreme, so here is a poem that released me from the depressed state of BREXIT. Brian is a kindly helpful person, so hopefully no offence given

Brian

He stood tall,

Knee length sky blue shorts,

With fetching chevron belt,

Silver glamorous shoes,

Shirt, salmon and cyan

Epitome of gayness

A bright Ray

Shining out on grey heads

His self-belief oozing

Beaming smiles over all,

Stentorian mumpsimus,

Kindly nevertheless

Walks in Old Age

Walking doesn't come easy now,

My fitness not what it was,

Right foot never seems part of me

When slugging through long green grasses

Easy it was a few years past

Out in the front striding along

Carefree, comfortable with life

Now puffing on the slightest rise

Others striding out before me

Leaving me behind in their wake,

Perseverance egging me on,

But at times there's the splendid view

Stiles present a challenge too

Straining getting my leg over

Then landing after a high drop

To stagger onwards, feeling my age

Glad to rest when we arrive

At a friendly inn where I sit

Drinking a cool lager beer,

Waiting for my fish and chips

Short articles about U3A Walks

*"The real world exists in the countryside,
where nature goes about her quiet
business and brings us greatest pleasure"*

Fennel Hudson

*"Au milieu de l'hiver, j'apprenais enfin qu'il y avait en
moi un été invincible."*

Albert Camus

" Some people walk in the rain, others just get wet"

Roger Miller

It was during April 2011 when the Walking Group of Northampton U3A spent a few days in the Cotswolds. We stayed at Harrington House at Bourton-on-the-Water and each day went walking on average ten miles a day. The weather was generally good and the particular poem I wrote during our stay there refers to one of these walks.

A Circular Walk from Harrington House, Bourton-on-the-Water

From the High Street in Bourton

Following the Windrush Way

Treading an old railway course time long forgotten

Admiring the flora come what may

English Longhorn cattle chew leisurely by a fence

Then by woods we sit, resting before a stiff climb

Away from the river passing old Lower Hartford lost in time

But anxious that he might miss his ale Tony is kept in suspense

In the valley below long Naunton lies

Where an old dovecote engages us for a time

Before venturing to the Black Horse Inn that Tony spies

Served by a landlady in flimsy dress, - divine

We say our goodbyes rather than dilly-dally

To leave sleepy Naunton all safe and sound

Taking the Wardens Way up out of the valley

Through parkland where old tumbled trees abound

Near to Hill Barn we stop for our lunchtime picnic

Soon stretched out lying under the hot sun

The grassy hillside and prickly hedge not too scenic

But Tony's reminiscences of his childhood rather fun

Following the River Eye to reach delightful Upper Slaughter

We linger in its churchyard behaving wisely

Not for us afternoon tea at The Lords of the Manor, - much laughter

Before pressing on to Lower Slaughter to arrive at three o'clock precisely

Many of us had ice cream at the old mill, - very working class

Others preferred tea on the lawn at Washbourne Court

And a goblet of white wine too at £9 a glass

But a pleasant ambiance made up for the bill, so not too distraught

Then it was back to Bourton by way of the Heart of England Way

Passing by the youth centre and library, its loveliest building

And on to Harrington House before we called it a day

To rest and shower and change for later dinning

Shropshire Walks, May 2014

From the lower slopes of the Long Mynd we gathered on a Saturday in May of 2014 at the Longmynd Hotel overlooking Church Stretton. The place was originally built as a Hydro in 1901 but didn't have any spa water and were told that this had to be shipped in regularly by rail consequently its popularity was short lived. But the surrounding location, known as Little Switzerland, has continued to attract many visitors over the years.

Church Stretton is built on a saddle between hills with streams flowing from it, both to the north and to the south, and is dominated by the Long Mynd to the west and Caer Caradoc and adjacent Stretton hills to the east. These hills have a fascinating history; about 566 million years ago imagine a place with volcanic islands set in a shallow sea located near the South Pole, a place then of fire and violent earthquakes. What is now Shropshire lay beneath this shallow sea in which lava and ash dropped on to it and eventually formed the Stretton Hills. Moreover, sedimentation was also laid down in the deeper sea and eons later these sediments hardened to form sandstone and shale rocks of the Long Mynd. The powerful nature of earth movement that has taken place over time, being in one of the major fault zones, although less violent now it still exists as the Church Stretton Fault. For instance, an earthquake of 5.2 on the Richter Scale was recorded in the 1990s. In the very distant past vigorous seismic activity has resulted in the steeply inclined layers of rock seen in outcrops today.

The hotel was our walking base for three whole days but the weather forecast wasn't good, heavy showers and cold winds. This short account of our walks in the area reflects my thoughts and impressions of this beautiful area of Shropshire, with woods and rounded green hills, some rising to over one thousand feet from the valleys below. I didn't take photographs on the long walks but my wife Cicely, who went on shorter walks did so and these are given here.

Chainsaw Sculptures

That first Sunday, I remember vividly, it was very windy with a grey overcast and some threatening black cloud. Behind the hotel at the top of the wooded grounds viewed some of the chainsaw sculptures set amongst the trees, taking particular note of a ring of bears standing on their hind legs. Afterwards took a path down through woods sheltered from the wind. Masses of white flowering ransoms lit up the surroundings and if you touched one a memorable smell of wild garlic aroused your senses. The trail led to the Old Ludlow Road and Little Stretton with its picturesque Victorian cottages and sixteenth century black and white timber framed houses. Cutting across the valley started to climb passing by a well looked after grave of a road accident victim, who died at the age of thirty. Such an abundance of flowers seen in the sheltered hedgerows were to become one of the features of the walks. Here a delightful mixture of bluebells, red campion and white stitchwort intermingled with grasses and other flowers. In a short time, after leaving the shelter of the village neighbourhood, emerged into open ground exposed to a howling gale blowing in from the southwest. A large hill rose before us at the 'Shropshire Way'.

Ragleth Hill is not a mountain, just a hill. Solid steps had been cut into the earth through springy grass aiding the walker. Followed the track of the footpath with its steps uphill, with a steepness of one in one. The severe wind made the ascent horrendous battling against regular gusts that attempted to blow you off your feet. At the top needed more layers of clothing to keep out the cold. As compensation, to the east had tremendous views over to the Clee Hills and Wenlock Edge. Pressed on to the north across the windy ridge rain hitting like needles on any exposed skin. Eventually descended the hill towards the east glad to get out of the relentless wind. The route onwards was along a narrow country lane whose banks were covered with flowers, which the 'Jack Mytton Way' followed to the southeast. Passing by Chelmik Farm turned down into the Chlemick Valley to the north and picked up a footpath that took us through a bluebell wood and down to the village of Hope Bowdler, with its namesake hill rising up above it. It was an opportunity to take an early lunch in the churchyard taking shelter under ancient yews from the wind and rain.

The rain had stopped by the time we set off again to climb the hill that has several summits. Ignoring these followed a footpath upwards along the line of Hope Batch and on reaching a plateau area headed northwards towards Wilstone Hill. In the distance saw a line of walkers with bright orange backpack covers descending it. These were teenage girls from Solihull on an outward-bound course, as part of their Duke of Edinburgh Award. They had made a mistake descending the hill and were glad to get information with regard to the direction they should take to the farm where they were to stay for the night. Not all the girls were keen on what they were doing and saw it as a necessary punishment to get the award on their CV, - how youth has changed. Climbing up to Battle Stones, looked back to see the girls disappearing in a line of orange following the course we had taken up from Hope Bowdler. From the rocky outcrop on the summit saw to the north a series of twisting valleys that descended to the Shropshire Plain punctuated by the unmistakable shape of the Wrekin.

After a brief rest retraced our steps down hill and looked over at Caer Caradoc with its iron-age fort and ancient settlement on top. It was the former home of that famous British chieftain captured by the Romans and renamed by them Caractacus. Dark clouds still moved across the leaden sky threatening more rain but fortunately experienced no more during the rest of the walk. A footpath took us around the western side of Hope Bowdler Hill to Gaer Stone then descended the hill to walk back to Church Stretton and climb up to the hotel.

After changing and showering went to the bar to get a drink and finish off part of a poem that was rumbling in my head about the climb of Ragleth Hill. A few days later finished off part two of the poem shown here in its entirety.

A Walk through the Stretton Hills

Part 1: Ragleth Hill

How beautiful the valley

Wild garlic beneath the trees

Our whispering voices carry

Hoping the strong wind will ease

Old timbered houses we pass

On the way to Ragleth Hill

Many bluebells in the grass

But the wind is far from still

At last our tough climb began

Heads into the treacherous wind

Following our leader's plan

Our feet to the hillside pinned

Gusting, blowing, eyes watering

Can we make the absolute top

There's no place for sheltering,

We're struggling and soon must stop

Plodding, shredding every nerve,

Knees weak and shuffling along,

How much will the weather serve,

The wild wind is much too strong

We reach the summit against the odds

Up six hundred feet from the bottom

Achieving it we must thank the gods

The fatigue we felt now forgotten

Walking along the bare grassy crest

Rain came in tempests of piercing pricks

Through grey curtains Long Mynd to the west,

Eastward Wenlock Edge and Clee transfix

Part 2: Hope Bowdler and Wilstone Hills

Pressing on through the blowing gale

Downhill to the Jack Mytton Way

Going eastwards towards Ape Dale

Then north to Chelmick Valley, hooray

Quiet from the blasting wind in a wood

With hyacinth scents and flowing stream

That refreshed our senses, doing good

Sheltered from that weather in extreme

Then quickly on to lunch at Hope Bowdler

In St. Andrew's churchyard under dark yews

While the congregation was still at prayer,

But of the weather had no better news

Climbing again high above Hope Batch

To reach a plateau between highpoints

Then on to high Battle Stones to catch

A fine view that never disappoints

To see as far as the Shropshire plain

And that outlying hill The Wrekin

Across the intervening terrain

Where grey rain curtains were closing in

Backtracking now to kind Hope Bowdler,

Westward Caer Caradoc darkly loomed

Its hill fort peak gave time to ponder

Its prince fought the Romans and was doomed

The track led to Gaer Stone above the town

From there descended to the Wenlock road

But took a footpath to continue down

To homely Church Stretton and our abode

The weather on Monday was much better, bright with sunny intervals, with much less wind and no rain. Started the walk from Castle Square in Ludlow and took a path around the castle walls to descend to the River Teme at the location of the nineteenth century three-arched Dinham Bridge. River noise from one of many weirs around Ludlow greeted us and was a reminder of Ludlow's industrial past when its many mills used the river's waterpower. The Teme is a fast-flowing river and before the weirs were constructed the noise from the river around the town gave the town its name, 'Lud', which refers to loud waters. Across the bridge turned off the road to follow a footpath westward along the line of the river crossing a field of tall meadow buttercups with some late flowering cuckoo flowers too. Here some orange tip butterflies were seen chasing pheromones flitting between the blooms.

Looking back the old castle stood out powerfully and saw why any invading Welch might have been put off going any further. The trail led past bluebell woods, with a blue haze spread beneath the trees, to reach the outskirts of Priors Halton. Afterwards had to negotiate two recently deeply cut ploughed fields with little consideration given by the farmer to walkers. The tiny village is more like a hamlet dominated by old farm buildings. The name probably refers to a Benedictine Priory that was once located hereabouts. From there a footpath led westwards towards Hill Hampton but instead skirted it to walk south to the wooded rising land of Lower Whitcliffe.

After a steep climb reached Killhorse Lane where to our right stood Mary Knoll House. A short way along the road took the way marker direction up the drive to the house then turned eastward to a wood, the trees spreading across the hillside of Mary Knoll. A short way through the woods left the footpath for an open grassy field to have lunch in a delightful scenic sunny spot.

After lunch returned to the footpath to continue on through woods to join the 'Mortimer Trail'. This led us down to Killhorse Lane again, but crossed over it to follow the trail down a steep incline to eventually reach Dinham Bridge. But instead of walking over the bridge into town followed instead the riverside walk around to Ludford Bridge. This is an old fifteenth century bridge that leads up into the town via Lower Broad Street, with its attractive Georgian cottages, some with potted plants standing outside, to reach an old town gate. This is the last surviving gate of the seven original medieval gates completed in 1270, but with many later restorations. The structure has two drum towers flanking a central passage. The best view is from the south when approaching it.

Castle at Ludlow

Passing on through the gate walked up Broad Street to take an outside table at a busy café situated in the high street near to the market square. While sitting sipping cool beers a bunch of cyclists from Liverpool arrived on expensive looking bikes. They had cycled from Landsend and were going on to John o'Groats; a lively bunch of lads who took most of what was left to eat in the café, as their support vehicle had broken down. After the break they were to go on to Shrewsbury for the night. There were about thirty of them and were doing it for charity. We said our goodbyes and wished them luck before leaving to look around the town.

The castle wasn't open but I remembered some of its history, the earliest period dating from the time of 'The Conqueror' and it's where the 'Little Princes' , sons of Edward IV, lived before being enticed to London to end their lives in the Tower. Taking an alley off the main square walked around to St. Lawrence's church, styled locally as the Cathedral of the Marches. This fifteenth century church with its elegant 41m tall tower was being restored bit by bit and as we talked about how well the stonework was done a man in a dog collar, seeing our interest, came to tell us more. I asked him about the plaque on the outside wall to A.E.Housman where flowers had been recently placed. He said this occurred, but infrequently. He told us the plaque was originally intended to be located inside the church until they discovered Housman was an atheist. Housman, who wrote the Shropshire Lad, is one of the country's best-known poets, but I could only recall at the time a verse that I often repeated to myself when in the area, and one remembered poem. Firstly, the verse that I have repeated often through the years

Clunton and Clunbury,

Clungunford and Clun,

Are the quietest places

Under the sun

The recalled poem below is haunting. As an older man Houseman looks back to his youth in early Victorian times. A very touching poem for those who are elderly. I believed it was his fortieth poem in the 'Shropshire Lad'.

Into my heart an air that kills
From yon far country blows:
What are those blue remembered hills,
What spires, what farms are those?

That is the land of lost content,
I see it shining plain,
The happy highways where I went
And cannot come again.

Feathers Ludlow

We walked on around the church to the impressive looking Reader's House. While I was admiring the carvings on the timber frame a man who lived next door, who was gardening, came over to me to chat about the place. The oldest parts he said dated from the 1300's but the majority of what remains is sixteenth and seventeenth century. Its history dates from the early church, to a wool merchant owner, and then, around 1430, was adapted as an early grammar school and lately is being used as the official residence for one of the local Clergy.

Pressed on down and through an old inn yard to see across the road 'The Feathers'. A timber-framed building that has a fantastic highly decorative façade. It was originally built in 1619 for an attorney in the town who practiced before the Council of the Marches when

Ludlow was effectively the capital of Wales. The building gets its name from the Prince of Wales feathers decoration on part the building. After the Civil War 'The Feathers' became an inn and has continued to this day as part of a hotel. Later went on around to that classical building, 'The Buttercross', which was built in 1746 and occupies a prime position in the town at the top of Broad Street. Its ground floor was originally a butter market while the town council used its upper floors, but today it is a museum. Later picked up the hotel's mini-bus at the top of Mill Street to take us back to Church Stretton.

It was a month later that I reflected on the experiences of the day plus others encountered in the March area and wrote the following poem

Through Woods and Over Hills

Pass through a county of curvy green hills

Enshrouded at times with enchanted woods

Hiding ruinous gems,

Like old Marcher castles

Seeking solace in the deepening shade

Press on through white carpets of wild garlic

Culinary delights

Crunching underfoot

Until emerge from trees to a bare hillside

Where, underfoot, springy grass eases tension

Luscious, delicate

Wild flowers enrapture

See for miles to misty distant plains

Blocked at times by other interceding hills

Enthralling, secretive,

Mysterious places

Where prehistoric man built his defences

Now moulded to a hillside in grassy banks,

- Concealed relics

Of an ancient past

On through more woods heavy with hyacinth scent

A blue shrouding contrasts with shades of green

Where Ill-fated intrigues

Reached a bitter end

Here remains of castle walls and gates

Guard a tumbled down keep now overgrown

With ivy and bramble

Hiding devastation

From a window in its walls see far and wide

Over a leafy valley with running waters

Noisily tumbling

In a boulder strewn gorge

Across a rickety bridge and up through trees

A rocky outcrop beckons from afar

To gaze upon wonders,

Cavorting butterflies

Amongst the many lilac cuckoo flowers

Where the orange tips fornicate for hours

Quietly reproducing,

In lasting engagement

Descend via the aged sunken drovers lane

Its banks illuminated by wild flowers

Bluebell, Red Campion

And White Stitchwort

Passed tumbledown woodsman's cottages

Almost buried by trees engorging on rock,

Hornbeam and hazel,

Majestic leafy oaks

Press on to that formidable castle

Silhouetted against the skyline

Dark and ominous,

Intimidating

Where the contiguous town gathers souls

To be ensnared for all eternity

Watching the woods and hills,

To see what stirs

The last day of walks started fine and sunny but deteriorated in the afternoon. Walked first through the rectory field, situated above the hotel, then by a footpath to cross the Carding Mill Valley Road to Madeira Way, an Edwardian development with fine views across the valley to Caer Caradoc. At the end of the cul-de-sac road continued along a footpath through trees that eventually took us to the top end of All Stretton where we turned away from it to go up Batch valley.

The road soon gave way to a track that continued on up the valley ablaze with sunshine. A coppice of hazel had a cluster of bluebells in the grasses and also hornbeams and distant hillside woods had bluebell spattered underlays creating much visual pleasure. Streams crossed the track in a few places with stepping-stones to ford them, or alternatively used bridges bypassing the fords. The track bent to the right near to the confluence of streams emerging from Long Batch valley and Jonathan's Hollow. Instead of taking the steeply ascending path to the top of the Long Mynd took a footpath up Jonathan's Hollow to make an easier climb. Passed by a modern prefabricated house situated in its own enclosure and wondered how planning permission had been given. It was in a spectacular spot with fine views back down the valley and snuggly tucked into the hillside with a coppice shelter. The footpath curved around to eventually join a steeply rising path from the valley to reach the top of the hill near to Jinlye, a small-holding.

Looked down on the lush green hillsides of the valley before turning towards a road that crossed the northern most part of the hill, but before reaching it turned towards the south along a track at 'Plush Hill', another small-holding. The weather had deteriorated, grey curtains of rain swept in from the southwest over the plain and saw that along the hill towards the gliding club dark clouds threatened. Carried on taking a footpath through bilberries and heather to Jonathan's Rock, an outcrop overlooking the valleys below. It is a wild treeless area, seemingly remote, but so near to civilisation. A sharp onslaught of hail rained down for a short time while pressing on around Jonathan's Hollow crossing over a dyke, one of the many remains of British Iron Age settlements found in the area. Walked on around Long Batch Valley towards The 'Port Way' but then turned off it to pick up Mott's road path to descend into Carding Mill Valley. Before the descent had a picnic lunch near to a small pond fed by springs. It was delightfully sunny and warm once more and sat back taking in the wonderful scenery with its long views

After the break for lunch it was a steep descent along a rough stony path to where the stream we had followed joined up with one emerging from Light Spout Waterfall. From there continued down to where the old Carding Mill is located and a welcome café. On the way passed groups of children from 'The Oratory School' carrying out various outdoor projects in and around the stream. While inside the café having drinks and cake it rained heavily, and thought so lucky to be inside in the dry comfort of the place.

Rain eventually cleared away and left the café to return to the hotel. On reaching the Burway Road took a footpath through Rectory Woods but on the way unfortunately got caught in another heavy downpour and had to take shelter under a large tree for a short while before walking on to the hotel to have drinks at the bar before the evening meal.

The short stay at Church Stretton had been a good experience with enchanting walks in the surrounding glorious atmosphere of the Shropshire landscape.

Winter Rambling

Trudging along the hedgerow mud sticks to our boots from the underlying wet clay and autumnal ripened grasses snag our legs.

"Only four and a half miles someone says".

"Yes, that's the usual", I reply

"Ten stiles already! Are we on a route march?"

"No, they're just to test you. You shouldn't grumble you have twenty more to go."

We head off across a freshly ploughed field, and climb over sodden great hummocks of earth and stone, soon our boots are laden with a sticky mess and the going becomes ever more difficult. Line astern advanced across the never-ending morass until at last reached the edge of the field and another stile that brings with it a welcome scraping opportunity. Unfortunately, others have been before and vast slabs of soggy dripping soil despoil the footrest.

Oh, forget about it, I say to myself there's another ploughed field on the other side of the ditch.

More waterlogged dirt makes it very heavy going with legs tiring fast and we haven't got half way yet.

Press on, I think to myself, the sooner we'll be through it.

Squelching through the mire and fetid pools we at last reach a grassy verge bordering a wood. I grab a fallen branch and break a bit off to scrape my boots. I feel much lighter already and raring to go on. Our leader cuts off down a path through the wood. It's murky inside and water drips down from the trees while underfoot a deep layer of fallen leaves not yet rotted down cushion our foot falls. It's quiet and eerie only the chatter of the women in the group stems the silence.

We had been walking just over an hour when our leader calls a halt for a break. The group takes off its backpacks and various items are fished out. Some drink from bottles and flasks while others munch on an apple, or banana and some discreetly sneak off into the depths of the wood to relieve themselves.

"Are we half way yet?" someone asks.

Of course not, I would be surprised if we had covered a third of the distance planned.

The break is finished after five minutes and not a moment too soon, as a cold wind finds its way through the trees at the edge of the wood. Everything is rapidly packed away, a seasoned rambler never leaves his or her litter, and backpacks are put on once more.

On we walk across a wooden bridge spanning a stream that runs alongside the wood and carry on over a field with stubble still standing from last September's harvest. Straw is strewn on the ground amongst the stiff stalks. A mixture of straw and clay is a well-known building material and in no time at all we are walking high above the field on elevated soles. To compensate, the view off the hill is stunning. Can see vast distances across the countryside making out church spires in neighbouring villages, a patchwork quilt of fields and woods that dot the landscape.

"Isn't that where we are heading for", says someone ever hopeful.

No, it isn't, where we are going is much further on beyond that valley and the wood we can see on the far hillside.

Several more stiles and muddy fields later passed through a kissing-gate to assemble together on the wide verge of a road. Our leader keeps us waiting there in the cold so that the stragglers can catch up, they are all strung out for at least three hundred metres with tail–enders not yet in sight. I lean back against the trunk of an old oak tree out of the wind thinking if some walked backwards their chatter might help to drive them on faster in the right direction by adding a jet propulsion impetus. At last, everyone is gathered together and the leader had donned his yellow waistcoat before we set off along the road. Not much traffic fortunately, but when a vehicle appears a raucous roar of "Car!" heralds its arrival in sight of the group. This helps those walking backwards to manoeuvre out of its way.

After half a mile along the road we turn right following the directions of the 'footpath' sign and climb what our leader says is the penultimate stile. Now in a field of lush green grass walking is pleasant, occasional fresh cowpats litter the ground adding interest and motivating strict avoidance procedures. Young heifers come trotting towards us fascinated with the strange animals ambling through their field. They gather around staring at us their wet shining noses dripping pints of saliva.

"I don't trust them", shouted someone.

"Don't be scared, they're only heifers and if you say boo they'll run off"

I walked over to them and they backed up, but became more intrigued with my presence. This gave the frightened group members chance to ease their way forward and run for the last stile. The rest of the group pressed quickly on with the heifers forming a strong counter move to push us fast to the stile, crowding in on us as the last member scrambled over.

Now in the lane to the village our pace quickened with a welcome prospect of the pub not too far away.

Arriving, eagerly changed out of our dirty boots before entering its warm interior, muscles recovering from their energetic exercise. Once in the bar we sat drinking and chatting awaiting our pre-ordered meals, happy and satisfied with our morning accomplishments relishing the atmosphere and in anticipation of good homely food, mud drying quickly on our trousers.

Somewhere a voice said, "That was never four and a half miles more like six according to my GPS."

I drank my beer and relaxed, thinking, distance is not important only the pleasure of finishing.

Striders, Christmas 2010 Walk

It was a cold crisp morning with a few frozen puddles underfoot from rain the day before. Frost crystals covered branches of shrubs and trees with a white Christmassy feel, as we set out from the Windhover pub, Chapel Brampton. A short way down the Brampton Valley Way a man stood by a gate that opened to a red-brown footpath that stretched out across white fields. On his gloved hand a raptor, hooded and with leg bells and jesses, clenched its claws, its brown feathers glistening. Our Leader, wearing his festive red hat with white fur trim, pushed through the gate with a nod to the attentive hawk. Following confidently, strode out towards a fast-flowing river, a northern branch of the Nene, and crossed it by an old red brick bridge where we stopped to look over at the rushing grey-white water filtered by a large knot of twigs and branches.

Walked on along the footpath and on over the tracks of main line of the north south railway, carefully observing the 'Listen and Look' sign. Our Leader was left on the wrong side, as a train appeared travelling fast. Taking courage he rushed across the tracks, as the train blasted its horn to cheer a scampering Santa. It was a good example of the 'Chicken Run', taking him back to his youth. Onwards again, and just before Grange Farm witnessed horses with back blankets galloping playfully in a large group emitting of vast amounts of steam that condensed in the cold air when they stopped. Passing by the farm headed towards the woods of Harlestone and Dallington Heath to a welcome shelter from the icy breeze. Crunching over the leaf-covered ground our leader picked out paths through birch and beech eventually heading downhill through trees towards the railway.

Much to our Leader's surprise the path through the tunnel under the railway was blocked due to engineering work as well as protection of plants of special interest. He was to remind us all later over lunch that it was very important for a leader to recce any walk just before the day of a walk, as anything may happen to stymy your plans: familiarity and past experiences are not to be trusted.

Walked back towards Northampton paralleling the rail track to the next tunnel along. Fortunately, the tunnel was open and all walked back on the other side along a rough frozen trail to the closed tunnel. It followed a fenced off area of cut down trees on the embankment to the railway, their yellowed wooden stumps creating a sorry sight.

Back on the right path again walked up hill through Fox Covert to the golf course of the 'Northamptonshire County Golf Club'. Traversed a deserted frozen waste to turn eventually along a track to Church Brampton. Passing through the village walked on taking a footpath that went past Brampton Hill Farm with a good view of the winter landscape and valley beyond. At a 'Five Way' finger post turned right along a hedgerow towards the village of Chapel Brampton where we spotted our sister group, 'The Ramblers', and caught up with them. Although it was only a short distance back to the pub two options presented themselves. Most of the 'Strider Group' took a short cut across the fields crossing the river further down, whereas the others, me included, crossed the river following Brampton Lane to the Northampton and Lamport Railway station to turn along the Brampton Valley Way once more.

Clouds had partly cleared and sunshine warmed us on the last leg and most walkers arrived at the pub together. A little later settled down to our excellent Christmas lunch and drinks, pulled our crackers, wore our silly hats and enjoyed ourselves to celebrate another fine year, our Leader well and truly thanked by all for providing us with such pleasure.

Ramble from Odell

Normally walk leaders will trial a walk a few days beforehand to refresh the navigation and to assess any difficulties. On this occasion I could only do the trial the day before. It turned out to be one of a 'Leader's' worst nightmares, as the council authority decided that very day to close the footpath for repairs and also as a consequence the bridge over the river leaving no alternative but to try another walk or to find a way around it. As there were 36 people on the walk late rebooking of a pub lunch was highly unlikely so the pub was fixed.

The day of the walk was fine and people gradually arrived at the Bell Inn Odell between nine forty-five only then to be told that they would have to drive on to Felmersham, the next village east down river where there was a bridge. However, the walkers must first order lunch at the pub. It was rather chaotic with an overfull car park and parking on the road outside, remarkably though everyone was soon on their way to find a suitable place to park near to St Mary's Church. Fortunately, the start of the walk was only delayed by a quarter of an hour from that on the original schedule. Soon everyone was walking up hill out of the village along the Pavenham Road out of the valley of the Great Ouse.

At woodland, skirting the road, a path cut westward along the ridge. Although there was sunshine the rain saturated ground left somewhat hazy distant views, which on good days are quite exceptional. Nevertheless, the going was good with a steady rambling pace, even though water lay on the surface under the path's grassy top pace. Pavenham's church spire showed just below the brow of the hill to the south.

The path eventually headed north-westward toward the right-hand side of Green's Spinney, where bluebells flower in profusion in springtime. Passing along the edge of the trees the valley of the Great Ouse spread out before us with the grassy path descending gently downhill. Towers and spires of several churches were clearly seen, with Odell's square tower straight ahead. Eventually the path met with the Felmersham to Carlton Road to turn left for a few tens of metres before turning again along a bridal path in a north-westerly direction. At a junction of footpaths turned right over a wooden bridge heading eastward along the valley, for if we carried on would have come to the construction work on the sluice gates at the Old Mill at the rear of the Bell Inn.

Many rabbit holes littered the edge of the narrow path and care had to be taken to not twist ankles. Black rabbits are sometimes seen hereabouts and are probably the result of inter-breeding with domestic ones. The river was still in flood on the north bank but our path followed higher ground, even at the riverbank where light brown rushes and grasses contrasted with the grey-blue turbulent waters of the river. Followed the path south along a hedgerow that led back to the road once more. Reaching it turned right up hill towards Carlton for a few hundred metres until reaching a narrow lane that headed south-eastward, not far from the Daisy Bank picnic site. Carrying on up a steady incline to reach the top of the hill had views of Odell and Sharnbrook. After a short rest climbed over a stile on the left-hand side of the lane where a path descended gently downhill over meadow land in an easterly direction towards double parallel gates. Passing through these gates headed diagonally across another meadow to the corner of the field where there were high hedges to climb over another stile into pasture. Eventually, came to the outskirts of Felmersham to cross two more stiles near to houses and walked back through the village to the church to change out of boots and drive back to the Bell Inn.

The luncheon arrangements at the Inn were good and the atmosphere friendly. The food good and homemade that made a fitting end to the unplanned outing.

Christmas Walk from Harpole

It had been sleeting when we set off from home and a little bit of drizzle still held on in the air, as we turned in to the car park of 'The Turnpike', a Beefeater we were to have our Christmas lunch later. A number of our fellow walkers were already there and changing into their walking boots.

When changed I joined the others for 'The Striders' walk led by Brian Adams. There were ten of us and we left a little late leaving the others to join Clive and Chris Spinney and on the 'Ramblers' walk that would set off about thirty minutes later. All were wrapped up in winter clothing and even I had four layers on against the cold, with the air temperature of about two degrees Celsius.

The first part of the walk took us up through the dormitory village of Harpole, not a pretty village especially on a cold dismal winter's day. The earliest spellings in the eleventh century for the village are Horpol or Horepol, indicating to some a derivation from horh, meaning dirty or muddy, and pol in both Celtic and Saxon meaning pool, very apt on the day, but I favour the derivation from the Saxon word Hor for bound, or limit. It was so cold we set off at a fast pace up out of the village trying to get warm, the older part much more attractive and a village mentioned in the Doomsday Book like so many in Northamptonshire.

Left the houses just short of Harpole Grange, taking a bridleway to climb a hill leaving the village below us. Streaks of blue sky showed in the west indicating an improvement for the weather to come, toiling up the steep slope with other rolling hills and woods to the west, an area termed the Northamptonshire Uplands. Soon, all gathered at the top taking a breather while Brian handed around for the first time many sweets from a plastic bag.

Heading in the direction of Nobottle Wood collected the first of sticky clay clods on our boots as we were drawn to the distant spire at Little Brington. Questions were asked about the spire and the origins of the name Nobottle. The first was easy to answer, according to Margaret, it was all that remained of a former church built on the Althorp estate. The main body of the church was demolished in 1947 after years of neglect, however at the request of the Air Ministry the idiosyncratic tower with its octagonal spire was spared, as it had become a landmark to navigators and probably still serves the same purpose today. The second question posed was much more difficult to answer, but probably the name is derived from a name meaning 'New Building' that probably refers to a 100 Meeting Place.

On reaching the old Roman road turned left along it keeping to the grass verge until reaching the first of two stiles to climb over to edge around Nobottle Wood before heading in the direction of Little Brington gathering more mud across crop planted fields. The

Brington's have their origins too dating back to Saxon times and perhaps even settlements of Celtic Coritani that date back even further. We stopped in the centre village for a halfway break when more sweets were passed around.

Lawrence Washington was a famous resident in the village having moved from Sulgrave Manor in 1610 when he sold the family home to his cousin Lawrence Makepeace, Lawrence Washington being the Great-great-great-grandfather of George Washington.

The weather had cheered up considerably with even some weak sunshine, to set off on the return leg passing by the old seventeenth century inn. It is called, 'The Saracens Head', and has a fine sign dangling outside.

Turned left by 'The Old Forge' with a date stone of 1749 to go down Blacksmith's Lane and then continued in a southerly direction on a bridleway that in turn merged to a byway. Brian said no more climbing, keeping the undulating hills to our left, it was downhill all the way to the Turnpike. This was his incentive to press on.

A few minutes later he led us up Glassthorpehill that has its highest point at 142m and did not continue on down to the topological remains of the deserted Medievil Village of Glassthorpe. On reaching the ridge had a fabulous view of the Nene Valley and beyond the visibility being extremely good, a good climax to our walk.

Having had our fill of peering at the landmarks and identifying them continued on along the ridge to a farm and from there descended off the hill to reach Glassthorpe Lane that took us all the way in to Harpole. The going was good and at a fast pace enabled us to catch up with the Ramblers in the village and beat them to the Turnpike.

Later had a merry and entertaining time for our Christmas lunch in a room especially laid out for us with two long tables. Over coffee and mince pies Clive set us his usual post lunch test to see how good our brains were functioning, then numbers were pulled out of a hat that had to be matched with pre-given numbers to collect a prize from a vast array of items contributed by group members. I think most people had at least something to take home with them. It was a good end to the year and all thanked Clive and Chris for their continued labour of love.

Walking Northamptonshire and surrounding counties

The simple pleasure of walking in the countryside cannot be surpassed; it's an expression of freedom as well as a medicine for the body and consciousness. So it is of no surprise that U3A's all over the nation have walking groups. These may go under different names, such as the three groups we have in the Northampton U3A, 'The Striders', 'The Ramblers', and 'The Strollers', but essentially they are all about enjoyment of the outdoors and the experience it brings, looking forward to a lunch and drink at the end of the activity and conversation during it, as well as the basic delights of life.

The three groups at Northampton are for people with different physical capability and walks are graded by mileage and obstacles: 'The Strollers' no more than 4km with preferably no stiles, but a few are permitted, 'The Ramblers' between 7km and 9km and 'The Striders' 10km to 14km. There are some walkers who are in all three groups just to get out more, for group activities are no more than once per month unless it is a special occasion such as a shared walking holiday, of which there has been more than one for the Striders and Ramblers and great fun too. The activities require a sharing of leadership throughout the year for there is much to planning a walk.

A walk has to be thought through using the appropriate Ordnance Survey Map for the area to be walked. An 'Explorer Map', which is 1:25000 scale (4cm to 1km) that indicates the field boundaries is extremely useful if the footpath signs on the ground are hidden or missing. One of the first decision points for a walk is the public house for lunch. This may be easy if there has been some past experience, but if it is a new area then it helps to have more than one option, so it is best to check out their webpages. Having found a suitable area for the walk the leader has to construct a walk on paper, preferably one that doesn't cross the same ground twice, a 'circular walk', or could be one with a small stretch of same ground walked twice commonly on the outward and inward stretch to the pub', a 'panhandle walk'. It is important to measure the distance using a map measure of some kind to be checked against the scale.

It is pleasurable exploring a new walk and discovering more about the landscape, the history of villages and hidden industrial gems. Northamptonshire and its environs have much to offer and is often called the county of 'spires and squires', with its woodlands, undulating terrain, grand houses, old churches, ancient villages bathed in English history and a hub for old stage coaching routes, canals and railways.

The feel of a walk will be different dependent upon the season and the weather. Sometimes paths may be overgrown and unsafe and stiles or gates a safety hazard and even checks the day before the Group Walk can be important. In the latter case I had experience of council workers closing the only bridge over the river Ouse for miles that necessitated a last-minute change of plan.

With regards to safety if you get the right contact in the Council it makes it so much easier. In preparing a walk out of the village of Stoke Goldington that is now within the political entity of Milton Keynes I discovered a very dangerous stile on a high bank and reported it to the people responsible for the Rights of Way through the Web and email. Within four days this stile was replaced by a kissing gate and with proper steps down the bank. This is probably the fastest action I have had but there is always action and stiles, gates and improved public access can be attained for the safety of walkers. Once a route has been checked out and timed it is time to ensure that the pub can provide for 'walkers' needs.

In these severe economic times, more and more pubs are closing and particularly badly affected are those owned by Brewery Chains who expect tenants to operate on slim margins. U3A walkers from all over help to keep these pubs alive, as well as supporting the Free Houses. If their food and service is good the venue may be used for further walks, or personal usage for lunch or dinner, it helps to spread the word.

Establishing good relationships with the landlord or landlady is important, for at times special favours may be required, such as an early opening for use of toilets and placing meal orders. Times for opening and expected arrival for lunch are given ahead of time, but the walk leader must confirm the likely number requiring lunch a few days before the start of the walk to allow the pub to make their necessary arrangements.

Weather on the day might be a problem but it is rare for a walk to be cancelled for the fickle British weather generally permits a go ahead providing the right clothing is worn. Walkers are always prepared and on the longer walks particularly in the summertime water must be carried. The changeable weather seasons enables the countryside to be seen in different ways. Sometimes farm animals may be a problem particularly for those who are nervous of such creatures. At one time the only way out of a field was via a stile surrounded by a herd of bullocks. Ingenuity is required to pave the way and allow the nervous to make their escape. At all the times the countryside code must be obeyed.

Walking through the countryside always brings with it a gain in knowledge, as well as improving physical fitness and the way we think.

Faces from the Archive

"In your wildest dreams you could not

Imagine that such things could happen to you!

Just wait and see!"

Roald Dahl

Prior to 2009

Dereck Hucker & Alan Walker

Roger Jackson, Dereck Hucker & Tony Sherwood

Hats at Brixworth

Malcolm Rea at Stanwick Lakes

Strollers Group

Strollers Queen Eleanor Cross Northampton

151

Linda Jackson & Chris Spinney investigating a tomb

Clive comes to inspect

Cotswolds Holiday

Cyril & Rona Cooper, at the hotel

Joanna Domhof, Linda Jackson & Chris Spinney

At the Pub (the walk described by the poem within)

Posh Tea

Tony & Joy Bishop & Roger Jackson

Not so posh tea

Eileen & Michael Brown

Not so posh tea

Group outside of Hotel Bourton-on-the-Water

On the walk described in poem

156

On the walk described in poem

Sue and Julia on the left

Printed in Great Britain
by Amazon